W9-BEN-596

The
Whale

Published by Raintree Steck-Vaughn Publishers, an imprint of Steck-Vaughn Company.

Acknowledgments
Project Editor: Helene Resky
Design Manager: Joyce Spicer
Consulting Editor: Kim Merlino
Consultant: Michael Chinery
Illustrated: Colin Newman
Designed by Ian Winton and Steve Prosser
Electronic Cover Production: Alan Klemp
Additional Electronic Production: Bo McKinney and Scott Melcer
Photography credits on page 32

Planned and produced by The Creative Publishing Company

Library of Congress Cataloging-in-Publication Data
    Crewe, Sabrina
    The whale / Sabrina Crewe; [illustrated by Colin Newman].
       p.   cm. — (Life cycles)
    Includes index.
    Summary: Describes the life cycle, behavior, and habitat of the world's largest animals, whales.
    ISBN 0-8172-4363-1 (hardcover). — ISBN 0-8172-6226-1 (pbk.)
    1. Whales — Juvenile literature.   2. Humpback whale—Juvenile literature.
3. Whales — Life cycles — Juvenile literature.   4. Humpback whale — Life cycles — Juvenile literature. [1. Whales.]   I. Newman, Colin, ill.   II. Title.   III. Series: Crewe, Sabrina. Life cycles.
QL737.C4C74   1997
599.5 — dc20   96-4846
                                             CIP   AC

1 2 3 4 5 6 7 8 9 0 LB 00 99 98 97 96
Printed and bound in the United States of America.

Words explained in the glossary appear in **bold** the first time they are used in the text.

LIFE CYCLES

The
Whale

Sabrina Crewe

RSVP ®

RAINTREE
STECK-VAUGHN
PUBLISHERS
The Steck-Vaughn Company

Austin, Texas

A baby whale is born.

Whales are born in the winter, in places where the ocean water is warm. A baby whale is called a calf. When a calf is born, it is 15 feet (5 m) long. It weighs nearly 3,000 pounds (1,400 kg)!

The mother whale helps her calf.

The mother pushes the calf to the surface
of the water as soon as it is born. The calf
must have some air. Although whales live
in water, they need air to breathe.

The calf is swimming.

The calf is three months old. It has grown quickly by feeding on its mother's milk. The calf swims by moving its tail **fin** up and down. The long **flippers** on its body help it balance and steer through the water.

The calf stays close to its mother all the time. If the calf is tired or sick, its mother holds it up so it doesn't drown.

The calf is part of a herd.

The herd is made up of many whales
who live in the same part of the ocean.
In the spring, the herd starts its journey
to colder waters.

The whales travel a long way every year.
This is called **migration**. The whales will
swim hundreds of miles without sleeping.

The calf travels with its mother.

The herd travels in separate family groups.
This is so there is enough food for all the
whales along the way. The mothers with
calves swim at the rear of each group.

The whales have arrived in cold waters.

There is plenty of food for the whales when they reach the cold waters. The calf is six months old. It has stopped drinking milk and is ready to feed on its own.

The whales are feeding.

The whales have **baleen plates** in their mouths instead of teeth. The whales take huge mouthfuls of water full of tiny fish and **krill**. Then they push the water out again, and their baleen plates trap the food.

The whale has made a bubble net.

The whales blow bubbles to make a circle around the krill. The krill are trapped in the middle. Then the whales can get them all in one mouthful!

The whale is as big as a truck!

The whale is **mature** when it is about nine years old. It will keep growing until it is 15 years old. The adult whales weigh around 80,000 pounds (36,000 kg) and grow over 50 feet (15 m) long. Sometimes they eat 3,000 pounds (1,400 kg) of food in a day!

The whales leave the cold waters.

The whales have spent the summer feeding in the cold waters. They have stored plenty of fat on their bodies for the winter. Every fall, the whales migrate again. The young adult males lead the way back to the warm waters.

The whales leap out of the water.

Whales race and dive together while they travel. They make huge jumps and crash down with a great splash. This is called **breaching**.

The whale is blowing.

The whale has come up for air. First it blows used air out of the **blowhole** on the top of its head. The air comes out and makes a big cloud of water droplets.

The whales are singing.

When they are in warm water, male
whales make wonderful sounds.
Sometimes whales sing alone, and
sometimes they sing with other whales.
The whole herd sings the same song,
but they change the song every year.

Whales can hear each other's songs
for many miles. The males may use
their songs to send messages about
where they are. They may be calling
for a female mate.

The whale dives and splashes.

When they are ready to mate, whales **court** each other. They hit the water with their tails. They play together in a group until they pair off with a mate.

The whale has found a mate.

The pair of whales swim side by side.
They will mate at the water's surface.
The female whale will give birth to a
baby 11 months after mating.

Whales need help to survive.

People have hunted whales for over a thousand years, because they wanted whale meat, oil, and bone. In the last hundred years, some whales have become nearly **extinct**. Now most people have learned to stop hunting and killing whales.

People can help whales by leaving them alone to **breed** more whales. They can try to keep the oceans clean for them. Then maybe whales will survive.

People are learning about whales.

Whales are the largest animals in the world. We know they are very **intelligent**. But how do they find their way across the ocean? What are they telling each other with their songs? How long do they live? There are still many things that people want to learn about whales.

Parts of a Whale

Whales live in water, but they are not fish. They are the world's largest **mammals**. Like all mammals, they breathe air and make milk to feed their young.

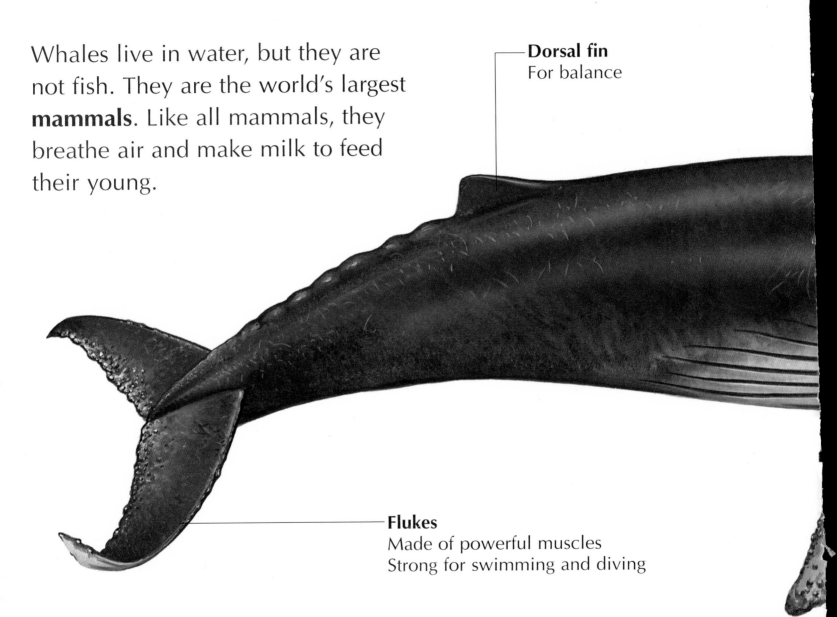

Dorsal fin
For balance

Flukes
Made of powerful muscles
Strong for swimming and diving

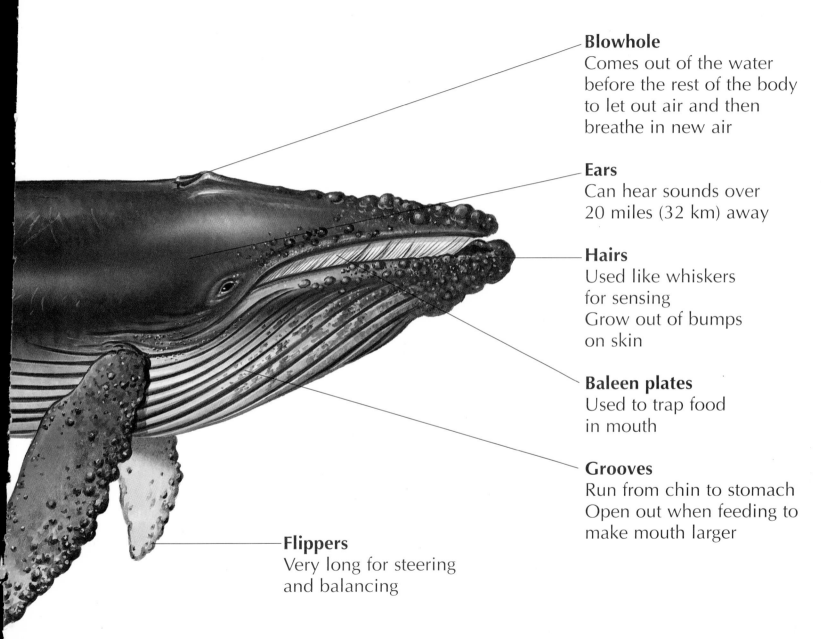

Blowhole
Comes out of the water
before the rest of the body
to let out air and then
breathe in new air

Ears
Can hear sounds over
20 miles (32 km) away

Hairs
Used like whiskers
for sensing
Grow out of bumps
on skin

Baleen plates
Used to trap food
in mouth

Grooves
Run from chin to stomach
Open out when feeding to
make mouth larger

Flippers
Very long for steering
and balancing

Other Whales

The whale in this book is a humpback whale. Most large whales have baleen plates instead of teeth, and they eat small **prey**. Smaller whales, such as dolphins and porpoises, do have teeth and can eat bigger prey. Here are some different types of whales. You can see how big they are compared to a person and to each other.

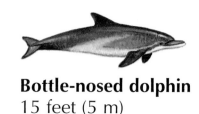

Bottle-nosed dolphin
15 feet (5 m)

Killer whale
30 feet (9 m)

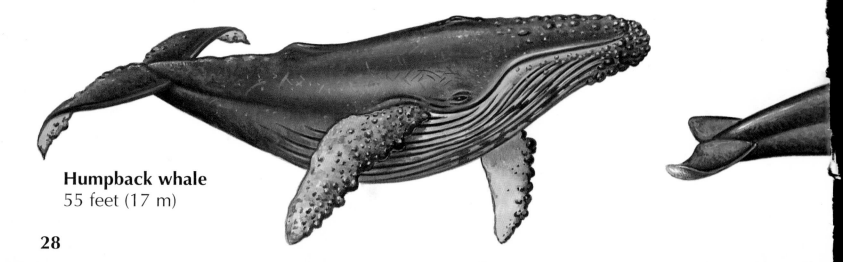

Humpback whale
55 feet (17 m)

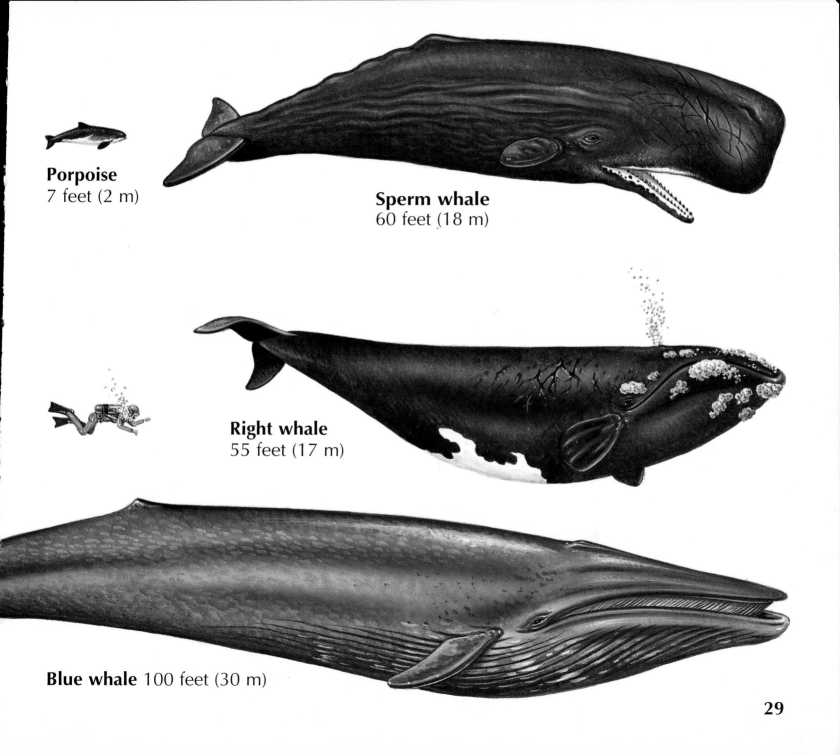

Porpoise
7 feet (2 m)

Sperm whale
60 feet (18 m)

Right whale
55 feet (17 m)

Blue whale 100 feet (30 m)

Where the Humpback Whale Lives

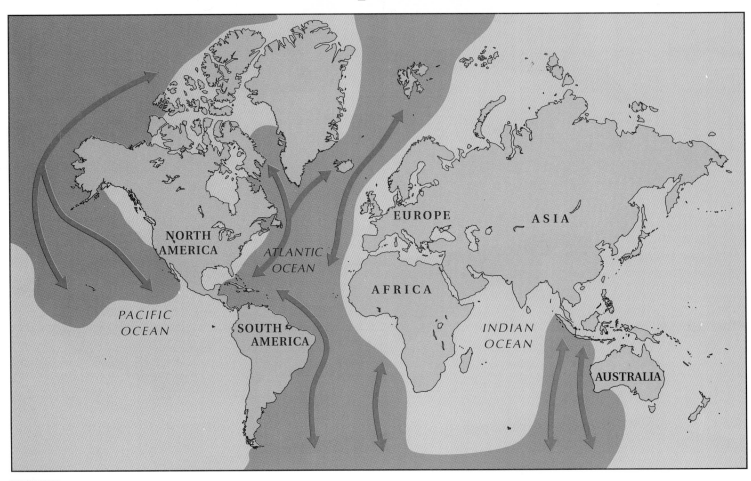

 Areas where the humpback whale lives

Migratory routes of the humpback whale

Glossary

Baleen plates The plates in a whale's mouth that strain and trap food

Blowhole The hole through which a whale breathes air

Breaching Jumping in and out of the water

Breed To mate and have babies

Court To try and attract another animal for mating

Extinct Something that has died out

Fin The thin flat part of a water animal that sticks out and is used for swimming or for balance

Flipper A winglike part of a whale used for steering and balance

Intelligent Able to learn and understand difficult things

Krill Tiny, shrimplike animals

Mammal A kind of animal that usually has fur and feeds its young with milk

Mature Fully grown

Migration The move from one place to another when the seasons change

Prey An animal hunted or killed by another animal for food

Index

Photography credits